1

M000120768

Gourmet Cowboy

Cowboy style gourmet cuisine

by Bob Kinford

Copyright 2009 by:

Too Lazy For You Livestock & Literary Co.

PO Box 815

Van Horn, Texas 79855

Website at http://gourmetcowboy.com

ISBN# 0-9660890-5-7

A Special Big "THANKS!"

I owe a lot to my wife Catie for allowing me to ignore her after working 12 to 14 hours a day so I could work on this book. Many of the ilustrations of *Cowboy Gourmet* are photographs taken in remote locatons I have worked at while the rest were created by Catie. You can see more of her art at www.ckinfordswest.com.

Last, but certainly not least, a big thanks to my mother who edited this book. Despite the fact she has been living with Parkinson's disease for over twenty years, she is still living a productive life and rendering assistance to others. She is an inspiration to every person she comes in contact with, whether they want her to be or not!

Foreword

Hollywood has perpetuated the myth that cowboys eat nothing but biscuits, beef, and beans. The fact remains, however, that cowboys are as omnivorous as a grizzly bear coming out of hibernation. After spending twelve to fourteen hours in the saddle, they are usually on their third or fourth helping before they figure out what they are eating.

Cowboys are also very pragmatic and are often considered the fathers of improvisation, making do with whatever resources are at hand. Whether it is being stuck afoot with a mad bull between him and his horse (with the bull being tied to the horse) or trying to make a meal for unexpected company when he is "out" of groceries, a cowboy has to figure out how to handle the situation.

The Gourmet Cowboy not only contains true gourmet recipes such as *Blackberry Quiche, Santa Fe Kiev* and *Surf In Turf*, it also has a special section dedicated to the improvisational qualities of cowboys: *Combinations (for those times you have "nothing" to cook).*

Each recipe is preceded by a paragraph or two describing how the recipe came to be...well more or less. Bob has a kind of twisted sense of humor. Some of the stories are true and some are a "little" stretched. You may have to watch yourself or you may start believing the wrong stories. Come to think of it, you may even just start reading and forget to cook....

Contents

Lamb   65

Seafood   74

Combinations   82

Vegetables   92

Soups Salads & Pasta   101

Deserts   120

MEASURING TABLE

Abbreviations:

tsp = teaspoon

Tbl = Tablespoon

c = cup

oz = ounce

3 teaspoons = 1 tablespoon

4 tablespoons = $^1/_4$ cup

6 teaspoons = 1 ounce

2 tablespoons = 1 ounce

1 cup = 8 ounces or $^1/_2$ pint

4 cups = 1 quart or 32 ounce

Beverages

Quench your thirst or warm up cowboy style

Cowboy Coffee

It is said that cowboy coffee is so stout it can float a horse shoe or dissolve your spoon. The truth of the matter is that it has a uniquely smooth flavor, although if not properly prepared, may be a little chewy (and will definitely boil over).

10 cups water
10 oz whiskey (optional)
4 T ground coffee

Bring 9 cups water to boil. Reduce to simmer and add coffee. Once grounds have quit floating, increase heat for one minute, bringing coffee to a boil and add remaining cup of water to settle grounds. Use one ounce of whiskey per cup for antifreeze.

Serves one cowboy or five normal people

Fridge Tea

Many people like to make "sun tea" by placing tea bags in water then setting it out in the sun. While this method does make a tea which is less bitter than boiling, there is an even better way. Just make it in the refrigerator! Not only is it ready when you get in after a hot day, it is already cold!

1 gallon water
4 "family size" tea bags
Place bags into water, them place into refrigerator.
Ready to drink in about three hours.

Makes one gallon.

Cowboy Cheap Chip Shot

A great drink whenever you are really cold. I was introduced to this one after spending nearly fourteen hours in sub-zero weather. Of course this is the cheap cowboy version.

1 oz peppermint schnapps
10 oz hot water
3/4 pkg instant hot chocolate

Mix hot water with your favorite instant hot chocolate mix, add schnapps and drink.

Serves 1

Cattle Baron Chip Shot

Cattle barons are no different than anyone else. They keep the good stuff to themselves. Compare this drink to the one on the previous page and you will see what I mean!

1 qt half and half

16 oz milk chocolate bits

8 oz Peppermint Schnapps

Place half and half into a 2 quart saucepan on

medium heat. Add chocolate and bring to a simmer,

stirring until chocolate is melted and blended

evenly. Remove from heat and add Schnapps.

Serves 6

Breakfast

Starting your day without breakfast is like trying to drive your pickup to town with no gas in the tank

Strawberry Quiche

If you are wondering why a cowboy would eat quiche, well it was by accident. I never knew what I was making until a city friend complimented me on how good my quiche was. By that time it was too late, I was addicted to them.

9" pie shell (see page 127)
10 oz frozen strawberries
3 eggs
8 oz whipped cream cheese
$^1/_2$ pt whipping cream
$^1/_3$ c unbleached flour
$^1/_2$ c sugar

Preheat oven to 410. Melt cream cheese in a microwave or double boiler. While cheese is melting spread berries evenly over the bottom of pie shell. Separate eggs, beating whites until they are stiff. In a separate bowl, whip cream until stiff enough to form peaks. Combine egg whites and cream, mixing on low; add egg yolks and sugar. Slowly sprinkle flour into this, then slowly add cream cheese. Continue mixing until all ingredients are well blended. Pour batter over berries and bake at 410 for 30 to 35 minutes, or until a knife inserted into the middle comes out clean. Let cool 10 minutes and serve.

Serves 4.

Blackberry Quiche

With Summer come the berries. Wading through the ocean of thorns, you hear the buzzing sound of rattlesnakes on either side of you while swatting mosquitoes off of your face and pulling thorns from your arm. Just when you think things could be no worse, a bear stands in front of you, licking berry juice from his lips. Not knowing what to do, you just stand there. The snakes and the bear leave and so do you. After you get home and have breakfast, the thorns don't seem to be so bad, and the bugs, snakes and bear seem to be less important - Breakfast sure was good and you are already planning another trip to the berry patch!

9" pie shell (see page 127)
1 c blackberries
8 oz whipped cream cheese
3 eggs
$^1/_2$ pt whipping cream
$^1/_2$ c sugar
$^1/_3$ c unbleached flour

Preheat oven to 410. Melt cream cheese in a microwave or double boiler. While cheese is melting spread berries evenly over the bottom of pie shell. Separate eggs, beating whites until they are stiff. In a separate bowl, whip cream until stiff enough to form peaks. Combine egg whites and cream, mixing on low; add egg yolks and sugar. Slowly sprinkle flour into this, then slowly add cream cheese. Continue mixing until all ingredients are well blended. Pour batter over berries and bake at 410 for 30 to 35 minutes, or until a knife inserted into the middle comes out clean. Let cool 10 minutes and serve.

Serves 4.

Hangtown Fry

This recipe originated in the town of Hangtown, California. In more civilized times, the name of Hangtown was changed to Placerville.

8 oz jar oysters
6 eggs
6 strips of bacon or links of sausage
3 Tbl evaporated milk
¼ tsp salt (optional)

Cook bacon or sausage until done, remove and drain. Brown oysters in remaining grease over medium heat. While oysters are browning, combine remaining ingredients and beat until mixture becomes frothy. When oysters are browned, drain off excess grease, if any. Add egg mixture and scramble to the consistency of your preference.

Serves 3.

Hanging Tree Quiche

This is the breakfast that the hangman of Carson City, Nevada had every morning during his off season.

1 9 inch pie crust (see page 127)
6 strips bacon
8 oz jar oysters
8 oz whipped cream cheese
4 oz diced green chili
$^1/_2$ pt cream
4 eggs
$^1/_2$ c flour
$^1/_4$ tsp salt

Preheat oven to 410.
Cook and drain bacon. Brown oysters in bacon grease. While cooking bacon and oysters, melt cream cheese in a double boiler or micro-wave. Whip cream until stiff. Separate eggs and beat whites until stiff. Whip egg yolks until they are foamy then combine yolks, whites and cream in a large mixing bowl. When bacon and oysters are done and have been drained, mix with green chili and spread evenly over the bottom of the pie shell. With the mixer on low, SLOWLY add melted cheese, salt and finally the flour. Continue mixing until thoroughly blended, pour into the pie shell. Bake at 410 for 30 to 35 minutes, or until a knife inserted into the middle comes out clean.

Serves 4.

Pancho Villa Omelet

Legend has it that the famous outlaw insisted on having this omelet every morning for breakfast. He claimed it had a magic which kept him one step ahead of his foes. On the day of his capture, it is said that Cookie substituted cheddar cheese for the cream cheese.

2 Tbl butter
3 eggs
2 tsp cream
$1/_2$ c cream cheese
2 oz chopped green chili

Melt butter in an omelet pan on medium heat. While butter is melting, combine eggs with cream and beat until frothy. Pour egg mixture in pan and cook until the top starts to solidify, then turn. Spread evenly with cream cheese and chili, cover and cook for one minute. Fold and serve.

Serves 1.

Snake River Berry Cream Cake

The Snake river is a beautiful winding river, cascading violently through rock-strewn canyons and spreading into wide quiet pools, back dropped by mountains poking their majestic peaks through the clouds. Along some of these pools you may find wild strawberries, one of these finds being the inspiration for this breakfast cake which may be topped with whipped cream.

1 pt fresh strawberries
2 Tbl butter
4 eggs
$1/_2$ pt cream
4 Tbl powdered sugar
$2/_3$ c flour

Preheat oven to 375.
Clean and slice strawberries. Place butter in a 9" pie pan and place in oven to melt butter. Combine eggs and cream and beat for two minutes with an electric mixer on high, or four minutes by hand. Remove butter from the oven and spread berries evenly over the bottom of the pan. Sprinkle powdered sugar evenly over the berries. Add flour to the egg and cream mixture slowly while mixing on high with an electric mixer, or by hand. Continue mixing with mixer for one minute, or two minutes by hand. Pour batter over berries and bake 20 to 25 minutes, or until a knife inserted into the middle comes out clean.

Serves 4.

Morning After Pancakes

Given to me by an old cowboy, this recipe is used to combat "Saturday Night Fever."   He claimed to never have a hangover when he ate these pancakes on Sunday morning. Guaranteed to be a tasty breakfast. No other guarantees or warranties expressed or implied.

12 oz. can or bottle of beer
2 c flour
$^1/_2$ c sugar
$^1/_2$ c water
2 well beaten eggs
2 tsp baking powder
2 pinches salt

Mix dry ingredients thoroughly. Add eggs, beer and water. Stir with a fork until mixture is well blended. Let batter set for five minutes. Spoon batter onto a well greased hot griddle or skillet. When bubbles begin to break on top of cake, turn and cook an additional minute.

Makes 10 to 12 six inch pancakes.

Hasharitos

This recipe was developed for those mornings when no one seems to have enough time to sit down and eat, and there is no place to pick up a breakfast packaged in styrofoam from some clown.

16 oz can corned beef hash
16 oz can refried beans
10 - 12" flour tortillas
8 oz grated cheddar cheese
8 oz fresh or frozen chopped green chili
6 eggs

Combine hash and beans in a skillet, heat over medium, stirring occasionally, until mixture begins to boil. While this mixture is cooking scramble the eggs. When eggs and hash mixture are finished, spread cheese evenly over tortillas. Next, spread hash mixture over cheese and add eggs, topping this with the chili. Fold one end of tortillas and roll.

Serves 5.

Beef

There are more old ranchers and cowboys than doctors...Could beef be the reason?

Wolf Creek Goulash

Wolf Creek, nestled high in the Rocky Mountains, is a sportsman's Paradise: Fishing in the spring and summer; deer, bear and elk hunting in the fall; and some of the world's best powder skiing in the winter.

3 Tbl butter
1 lb beef fondue meat
1 small onion
1 small bell pepper
8 oz mushrooms
4 oz can diced green chili
10 oz burgundy
1 tsp garlic salt
10 oz pkg vermicelli
4 oz cream cheese
4 oz relyeta cheese

Melt butter in a skillet over medium heat and brown meat. While meat is browning, wash and chop onion, bell pepper and mushrooms. When meat is browned, add vegetables, burgundy and garlic salt. When mixture reaches a full boil, lower to a simmer and cover for ten minutes. While mixture is simmering, prepare vermicelli as per package instructions. When meat mixture has simmered for ten minutes, slice cheeses over the top and recover for five minutes. When vermicelli is finished, drain and mix into the meat.

Serves 4.

Pie Place Goulash

After working twelve to fourteen hours on a branding crew, and having to cook for several hungry cowboys, you come up with some quick dishes such as this one. At the time of this dish's origination, I was working on the Pie Ranch and had four to eight cowboys to feed twice a day in addition to being horseback for twelve to fourteen hours a day.

8 oz egg noodles
1 lb hamburger
1 medium onion
16 oz can mixed vegetables
8 oz sour cream
4 tsp paprika
2 tsp garlic powder
$^{1}/_{2}$ tsp salt
1 tsp black pepper
1 tsp ground sage

While noodles are cooking, peel and chop onion. Brown onion and hamburger. When noodles are finished drain, and add to meat and onion. Add vegetables, without draining, and rest of ingredients. Bring to a simmer and serve. Takes approximately fifteen minutes.

Serves 4.

Spokane Goulash

This was a dish used to feed a hungry cattle buyer from Spokane. He was rather ill-tempered upon his arrival at the ranch, so I fed him before showing the yearlings. He ended up in a better mood and paid top dollar for the herd.

1 lb hamburger
12 oz burgundy
8 oz cream cheese
6 $^1/_2$ oz jar artichoke hearts
4 oz jar pimentos
1 Tbl dried onion
10 oz shell macaroni

Prepare macaroni as per package instructions. While macaroni is cooking, brown and drain hamburger. Add all ingredients, except macaroni, to hamburger, placing cream cheese on top. Bring to a boil, reduce to a simmer and cover for ten minutes. Drain macaroni, mix into the meat mixture and serve.

Serves 4.

Mongolian Rim Goulash

Camped at timberline on the Mongolian Rim, with the smell of an aspen fire and a full moon overhead, reflecting the shadows off the freshly fallen snow is how this recipe came to be.

12 oz can evaporated milk
1 small onion
2 Tbl butter
5 oz jar dried beef
8 oz cream cheese
$^1/_2$ c burgundy
4 oz can chopped green chili
1 lb hamburger
$^1/_2$ c burgundy
8 oz cream cheese
6 $^1/_2$ oz jar artichoke hearts
4 oz jar pimentos
1 Tbl dried onion
10 oz shell macaroni

Prepare macaroni as per package instructions. While macaroni is cooking, brown and drain hamburger. Add all ingredients, except macaroni, to hamburger, placing cream cheese on top. Bring to a boil, reduce to a simmer and cover for ten minutes. Drain macaroni, mix into the meat mixture and serve.

Serves 4.

Tahoe Goulash

The idea of eating heart is not appealing to some, yet it is actually one of the best cuts of meat. It has a delicate flavor, a tender texture and is very lean. Health wise, it is probably the best cut of meat you can eat.

1 lb beef heart
12 oz can evaporated milk
2 Tbl butter
1 bell pepper
6 green onions
6 oz can pitted black olives
$^1/_2$ c port wine
4 $^1/_2$ oz can mushrooms
1 tsp garlic salt
2 tsp cornstarch

Cut heart into bite sized pieces and brown in butter. While heart is browning, chop onion and bell pepper. When meat is browned add remaining ingredients, reserving $^1/_2$ of the evaporated milk and cornstarch. Bring to a boil, reduce heat, cover and simmer for twenty minutes. Blend evaporated milk with cornstarch until smooth. Add this to the meat mixture and stir for one minute. Serve over rice or egg noodles.

Serves 4.

Magdalena Meat Loaf

Magdalena is a small town in New Mexico that has produced people who have left town to become successful businessmen and ranchers, making and sometimes losing millions of dollars (only to make it back). For one weekend every summer, the town of a few hundred swells to several thousand for the annual rodeo.

$1^1/_2$ lb hamburger
4 oz grated cheddar cheese
4 oz diced green chili
1 small onion 6
1 Tbl flour
4 Tbl sour cream
3 Tbl red chili powder

Preheat oven to 350. Chop onion. Combine all ingredients until they are thoroughly mixed. Pack into a bread pan and bake at 350 for $1^1/_2$ hours.

Serves 4.

Sweetwater Pot Roast

This recipe originated on the banks of the Sweetwater River. The original recipe used elk and was cooked in a dutch oven over an open fire.

3 to 4 lb pot roast
28 oz can peeled tomatoes
1 eggplant
4 strips bacon
1 Tbl lemon pepper seasoning
10 ½ oz can cream of mushroom soup
10 ½ oz can chicken broth
4 carrots
4 stalks celery
1 large onion

Brown roast in a large roasting pan. While roast is browning, cut bacon into thirds, chop onion and celery and carrots. When roast is browned, add bacon, onion, carrots and celery. Sprinkle with lemon pepper seasoning, then add soups and tomatoes. Cover and cook over medium heat 1 ½ to 2 hours. Ten minutes before serving, cut eggplant into quarters length wise, then cut the quarters in half and add to the roast.

Serves 6.

Borderline Pie

This recipe was adapted from whatever ingredients were handy. I was about ready to run into town for supplies when unexpected company showed up, (when you live beyond the phone lines, most company is unexpected) and as usual they were hungry.

1 lb hamburger
2 tsp garlic powder
3 Tbl red chili powder
1 large onion
8 oz sour cream
8 oz mayonnaise
6 oz chopped black olives
8 oz chopped green chili
2 medium tomatoes
2 - 9" pie crusts (see page 127)
12 oz grated longhorn or Colby cheese

Preheat oven to 350. Brown hamburger with garlic and chili powder. While meat is browning, chop onion finely and mix well with sour cream, mayonnaise, black olives and green chili. Slice tomatoes as thinly as possible. When hamburger is browned, drain and place evenly into pie crusts. Place a layer of tomato slices, then a layer of mayonnaise over both pies topped with another layer of cheese. Bake at 350 for 30 to 35 minutes. Let cool five minutes before serving. MAY BE FROZEN AND BAKED AT A LATER TIME. After freezing increase cooking time to 45 to 50 minutes. Each pie serves

4 to 6.

Quick Rib Stew

This recipe came about after ten hours in the saddle looking for a wild bull. The bull was spotted, but it was too far off to get a rope on.

6 to 8 beef ribs
1 c flour
6 carrots
1 large onion
24 oz evaporated milk
16 oz can whole white potatoes
10 ½ oz can cream of mushroom soup
1 tsp garlic salt
½ tsp sweet basil
½ tsp rosemary
½ tsp white pepper

Roll ribs in flour and brown. While meat is browning, cut tops from carrots and cut in half. Peel onion and cut into bite sized pieces. When the meat is browned, place in the bottom of a one gallon pot. Add vegetables and sprinkle spices over the top. Add cream of mushroom and evaporated milk. Cook over medium heat for 30 minutes.

Serves 3.

Teton Tips

This recipe originally used venison from a hunting trip on the west slope of the Tetons. Great meal no matter what you have been doing in the cold all day.

1 lb sirloin tips
8 oz mushrooms
1 small onion
1 medium bell pepper
8 oz cream cheese
10 $^1/_2$ oz can beef consommé
$^1/_2$ c port wine
2 cloves garlic
2 bay leaves
$^1/_2$ tsp salt

Brown meat in a large skillet. While meat is browning, slice mushrooms, chop onion and bell pepper into quarter inch slices. When meat is browned, add all ingredients and simmer for twenty minutes. Serve over rice, noodles, toast or warmed corn tortillas.

Serves 4.

Box Canyon Stew

Prepared for the first time in a dutch oven, this recipe came about while trapping wild cows in a box canyon which contained the only water for a twenty mile radius.

3 lb pot roast
20 oz teriyaki sauce
4 carrots
8 asparagus spears
8 oz bamboo shoots
4 oz bean sprouts
4 oz snow peas

Brown roast. When roast is browned, add teriyaki sauce, cover and simmer for two hours. Slice carrots and add all remaining ingredients to meat. Cover and simmer ten minutes. CAUTION: do not over cook the vegetables or the teriyaki sauce will over power their flavor.

Serves 4.

Sicilian Pot Roast

Some people will believe almost anything; or rather fail to grasp the most obvious. When I was in Air Force basic training, a man from New York City asked me if I actually rode horses, roped and branded cows before I joined up, to which I replied to the positive. When he stated that he did not realize that sort of thing still took place, I asked him where he thought the hamburger he had just eaten for lunch came from. He replied, "From a factory." This recipe is dedicated to my Italian friend from New York City.

3 lb pot roast
1 large onion
2 large potatoes
1 large clove garlic
$^1/_2$ tsp sweet basil
$^1/_2$ tsp marjoram
$^1/_2$ tsp oregano
$^1/_2$ tsp rosemary
10 $^1/_2$ oz can French onion soup
1 - 28 oz can peeled tomatoes
5 oz sauterne
2 small zucchini

Brown the roast in a large pot. While the roast is browning, cut the onion into eighths, the potatoes into quarters and the garlic into small slivers. When the roast is browned, add potatoes and onion, then sprinkle the spices on top. Pour the soup over the spices, then add sauterne and top with tomatoes. Cover and cook over medium heat for 1 $^1/_2$ to 2 hours. Slice and add zucchini during last 10 minutes of cooking.

4 to 6.

Brandied Beef

I was trying to impress a lovely lass when I developed this potential bonfire. As the meat was cooking and my lady friend was cooking a side dish, I received a call from my boss. In the middle of discussing the condition of the cattle, my eye caught black smoke billowing from the grill. Without missing a beat in the conversation, I started jumping up and down, pointing out the window, at which my lovely companion merely gave me a sexy smile and waved back with the knife she was using. Upon completing my conversation I promptly ran out the door to salvage the meat. Skewering the meat with a large fork, I brought the remains into the house. "This is what I was jumping and pointing at", I said to my friend, as her jaw dropped at the sight of the still flaming cremation. From the one bite of salvageable meat I could tell this was a good recipe (as long as you could keep from burning the place down!)

3 to 4 lb chuck roast
4 c Brandy
2 c brown sugar
2 tsp cinnamon
2 tsp ground allspice
Place roast into a shallow pan and sprinkle with sugar and spices. Pour Brandy over the top, cover and refrigerate for 4 hours. Turn roast over and refrigerate an additional 4 hours. Cook over coals or low heat on grill to your preference.

Serves 4 to 6.
(CAUTION: THIS RECIPE IS FLAMMABLE. WATCH CLOSELY)

Savory Lemon Steak

Team penning used to be of my favorite pastimes. In this sport, a team of three riders goes to the far end of the arena and attempts to cut out three numbered steers and put them into a pen at the opposite end of the arena. While this may seem to be a strange way for a cowboy to spend his day off, on a horse chasing cows, it is great fun and an opportunity to socialize. This dish was concocted to barbecue for lunch during these gatherings.

1 $\frac{1}{2}$ lb beef loin steak
1 c red wine
1 Tbl lemon pepper
1 tsp summer savory
$\frac{1}{4}$ tsp garlic powder
1 bay leaf

Place beef in a shallow container and sprinkle with spices. Place bay leaf on top and pour in wine.   Cover and refrigerate four to six hours and grill to your preference.

Serves 3.

Fifth Try Stew

The older you get the better chance you have of making a marriage work because you don't have as much time to have things go wrong. This stew was created for the fifth wedding of a good friend of mine, and talking about situating yourself; he has done good. Walter's fifth wife not only happens to be twenty years younger than himself, she also happens to be a nurse, which makes his daughter very happy as now she doesn't have to worry about him as much when he falls off his horse.

4 lb beef stew meat
4 - 16 oz cans white potatoes
32 oz water
1 - 16 oz package frozen carrots
1 large onion
4 Tbl dried parsley
4 Tbl powdered beef bullion
2 tsp dry crushed red pepper
1 tsp dry crushed basil leaves

Brown beef in a large dutch oven or pot. While beef is browning peel and chop onion and garlic. When beef is browned add remaining ingredients and bring to a boil, then reduce heat to a simmer for 30 minutes.

Serves 12 to 15.

Pork

Make everyone squeal with delight at the other white meat

Why Chops

Why are these chops named Why? Because they are named after the small town of Why, Arizona. There is no question as to how Why got its name. The only question is why a town would be located where Why is.

4 center cut pork chops
3 Tbl chopped green chili (fresh or frozen)
1Tbl fresh chopped cilantro
1 tsp paprika
$^1/_2$ tsp garlic powder
$^1/_2$ tsp ground coriander
Preheat oven to 350.

Holding the chops on edge with bone side down, cut as if filleting down to the bone. Reserving paprika, mix the chili and spices, then stuff the chops and place in a shallow baking pan. Sprinkle paprika evenly over the meat then bake for 30 minutes at 350.

Serves 2.

Outlaw Ribs

This is a favorite dish of pork rustlers everywhere. With it they celebrate another successful raid while destroying the evidence.

2 $^1/_2$ lb country style spare ribs
Juice from 1 grapefruit
2 Tbl sugar in the raw
2 Tbl brandy
2 Tbl vinaigrette dressing

Combine juice, sugar, brandy and vinaigrette in a small saucepan over medium heat, stirring constantly until sugar is dissolved. Place meat in a mixing bowl, pour sauce over meat, cover and refrigerate for 3 to 4 hours. Cook over charcoal fire or gas grill.

Serves 4.

Aspen Meadow Chops

These chops were first prepared in a hunting camp located in an aspen meadow high in the Rocky Mountains.

6 center cut pork chops
$^1/_2$ c Sherry
8 oz mushrooms
1 small white onion
2 Tbl olive oil
1 tsp summer savory
$^1/_2$ tsp salt
$^1/_4$ tsp fresh ground black pepper
$^1/_4$ tsp ground clove
2 c water
2 Tbl cornstarch

Brown chops in olive oil. While meat is browning, clean and slice mushrooms, peel and chop onion. Once meat is browned, add remaining ingredients RESERVING cornstarch and one cup water. Cover and simmer 25 minutes. Remove meat from sauce. Combine reserved cornstarch and water, stirring until smooth. Stir this mixture into sauce and simmer until thick. Serve over rice or pasta.

Serves 3.

Blue Ribbon Pork Chops

This recipe was developed as an easy meal to prepare after a horse show. It is simple to prepare and takes less than half an hour from start to table.

1 $1/_2$ lb boneless pork loin chops
2 Tbl olive oil
5 scallions
4 oz fresh mushrooms
1 c sauterne
$1/_2$ tsp sweet basil
6 whole allspice
1 c cream
1 Tbl cornstarch

Brown chops in olive oil. When meat is browning, slice scallions in thirds and cut mushrooms in half. When meat is browned, add remaining ingredients, reserving cornstarch and cream. Cover and simmer twelve to fifteen minutes, or until wine has nearly evaporated. When wine is nearly evaporated, blend cornstarch with cream until smooth. Remove meat, replacing it with the cream mixture and stir over medium heat until it begins to thicken. Serve with cream sauce over chops on bed of rice or pasta.

Serves 2.

Spear Burritos

This recipe is dedicated to the primitive people who were forced (and in some areas are still forced) to hunt their meat with a bow and arrow or spear.

2 Tbl olive oil
12 oz diced pork
2 Tbl red chili powder
4 large flour tortillas
4 oz can diced green chili
4 Tbl sour cream
4 Tbl grated cheddar cheese

Stir fry pork in olive oil with red chili. When pork is well browned, add green chili. Continue stirring until this mixture is hot. Divide this mixture evenly between the tortillas, next placing sour cream and cheese over meat and chili. Fold one end of the tortilla up over the stuffing to create a closed end, and then roll.

Serves 4.

A #2 Spare Ribs

While working on the Ponderosa I met Hop Sing's cousin, a famous hog slopper by the name of Slop Sling, whom I pilfered this recipe from. While it is delicious fresh, the combined flavors of this sauce are best if refrigerated overnight before cooking ribs. (This sauce is also excellent on beef or chicken...)

5 lb pork spare ribs
1 medium red onion (finely minced)
2 -15 oz cans tomato sauce
1 c honey
$^1/_2$ c brown sugar
$^1/_2$ c burgundy
$^1/_4$ c concentrated lemon juice
2 Tbl olive oil
2 Tbl Dijon mustard
1 tsp salt
1 tsp garlic powder
1 tsp black pepper
1 tsp allspice
1 tsp Worcestershire sauce

Sauté onion in olive oil until clear. Add remaining sauce ingredients and bring to a boil, stirring sauce constantly. Reduce to a simmer for ten minutes, stirring occasionally. Grill ribs for four hours on indirect charcol heat turning and basting with sauce every thirty minutes.

Serves 6.

Diamondback Stir-fry

This is another favorite recipe of Slop Sling which he would make on cattle drives out of Diamondback Rattlesnakes to ensure that all of the cattle would make it to market.

1 lb pork stew meat
8 oz pkg oriental noodles
$^1/_2$ head cabbage
1 bell pepper
1 medium onion
8 oz mushrooms
2 carrots
4 tsp sesame oil
$^1/_2$ c water
16 oz can fruit cocktail
1 tsp hot mustard powder
1 tsp ginger
1Tbl Arrowroot

Prepare noodles as per package instructions. Chop vegetables. Brown pork with sesame oil in a wok on high heat. Add vegetables and water, cover and cook three or four minutes or until most of the water has evaporated. While meat and vegetables are steaming, reserve $^1/_2$ of the juice from the fruit cocktail. Combine the remaining juice, along with the fruit, hot mustard powder and ginger in a saucepan over medium heat. Blend the Arrowroot with the reserved juice until smooth and stir into the fruit mixture until it begins to thicken, then remove from heat. Place meat and vegetables over noodles and top with sauce.

Serves 5.

Wolf Creek Chops

While fishing Wolf Creek, we discovered Steve's wife had mistakenly packed some pork chops in with the beer. I was forced to cook them as we caught none of the fish we were expecting to eat.

4 shoulder cut pork chops
10 oz can cream of mushroom soup
4 Tbl butter
4 oz can diced green chili
1 c evaporated milk
$^1/_2$ tsp salt
16 oz can white potatoes

Brown chops in butter. While meat is browning, mix all ingredients except potatoes. When meat is browned, drain potatoes and add to meat, pour remaining ingredients over top. Cover and simmer fifteen minutes.

Serves 4.

Poultry

The early bird may get the worm, but the early worm becomes breakfast

"Doctoring Birds"

Injecting poultry with wine, butter and other ingredients insures against ever having a "dry" bird, and also increases the variety of flavors you can give a simple chicken. Since the natural juices of the bird are held inside, poultry may appear under cooked, even though you inadvertently left it in the oven too long.

When injecting poultry use flavor injectors, available in gourmet shops, or go to a feed store and buy a 20 cc syringe and a 14 gauge needle, which is what I have used for years. Inject the bird in the muscle, next to the bone with half of your basting, and inject the other half just under the skin, making sure to distribute baste fairly evenly throughout the bird.

The desert is the last place one would expect a pelican...but here they are, lost again!

Balls'O Fire Peach Chicken

This recipe is an elegant main course adapted from an old family recipe. The adaptation came when my great-aunt Myrtle slipped in the kitchen spilling her drink of orange brandy over the stove. Luckily the house did not burn down, and it improved the chicken.

2 lb boneless chicken breast
16 oz can sliced cling peaches
$^1/_2$ c peach brandy
3 Tbl olive oil

Preheat oven to 350. Brown chicken in olive oil. Place in a shallow baking pan and add peaches, pouring juice over chicken. Bake for 20 minutes at 350. Pour brandy over chicken and light; serve when fire dies.

Serves 4.

Thankful Turkey

The fear of all turkeys is that they will wind up dry, resembling a dehydrated "just add water" meal, without the water, rather than the moist delicacy enjoyed by the Pilgrims. To help alleviate this fear, and have the turkeys flocking to your house for Thanksgiving dinner, just follow this moisture guaranteed recipe.

20 lb Turkey
750 ml bottle Chablis Blanc
14 oz pkg bread stuffing mix
$^1/_2$ lb butter
8 oz pkg sliced mushrooms
1 c walnuts
1 onion
2 Tbl honey
2 Tbl dried summer savory
$^1/_2$ tsp garlic juice
$^1/_2$ tsp onion juice

The night before cooking the bird, pour the Chablis into a saucepan, wrap summer savory in a coffee filter and secure with a piece of thread. Cover for the night. Remove summer savory from Chablis (reserving savory for stuffing) and add butter, garlic juice, onion juice and honey to Chablis. Inject this mixture evenly throughout bird. Melt remaining butter over low heat.

While butter is melting chop onion. When butter is melted add onion and sauté until clear. When onion is clear combine this mixture with stuffing mix, walnuts, mushrooms and summer savory. When this mixture is well blended, loosely stuff body and neck cavities of the bird, tie legs together. Cover and roast for 5 hours on 350. After 4 hours, remove cover and cook for an additional hour or until the wings remove easily when pulled.

Serves 8 to 10.

Giblet Gravy

Moisten those dry potatoes

Neck and "innards", minus liver from above turkey.
8 c water
4 Tbl cornstarch
1 tsp crushed red pepper

Combine turkey parts, red pepper and $7\,^1/_2$ c water in a saucepan. Cover and bring to a boil. Reduce to a simmer for about two hours or until there is approximately 4 cups of water left. Remove turkey parts from broth. Combine cornstarch with $^1/_2$ c cold water and mix until there are no lumps. Bring broth to a boil, add cornstarch mixture, stirring constantly until mixture begins to thicken. Remove from heat.

Makes 5 cups gravy.

Confucius's Confused Quiche

This recipe was developed especially for an ex-girlfriend's psychiatrist who claimed she was emasculating the men in her life by refusing to cook for them. For her next appointment she presented him with a piece of this quiche and an unidentifiable object which she had cooked. Needless to say he changed his mind about her need to start cooking.

9 inch pie crust (see page 127)
$^1/_2$ lb boneless chicken breast
$^1/_2$ pt whipping cream
$^1/_2$ c mixed nuts
$^1/_2$ can chop suey vegetables
3 eggs
4 oz cream cheese
$^1/_8$ c flour
2 Tbl sesame oil
1 Tbl honey
1 tsp crushed red pepper
$^1/_2$ tsp garlic salt
Preheat oven to 410.

In a hot wok, stir fry chicken in sesame oil with mixed nuts, honey and red pepper. When chicken is done, remove from heat. Melt cream cheese in a double boiler. While cheese is melting, whip cream until stiff, separate eggs and beat whites until stiff. Spread chicken mixture evenly over the bottom of the pie crust and top with chop suey vegetables. Beat egg yolks until foamy and blend with garlic salt, mix in cream cheese. Fold egg whites and cream into this mixture until well blended, then slowly blend in flour a little at a time. When flour is well blended into this mixture pour batter into pie crust and bake at 410 for 25 to 30 minutes or until a knife inserted into the middle comes out clean.

Serves 4.

Rocky Mountain Savory Chicken

This savory recipe was first concocted in a cow camp on the Continental Divide in Colorado. Although grouse was used in the original, chicken substitutes very well, especially when served over a bed of wild rice.

$1^1/_2$ lb boneless chicken breast

$^3/_4$ c water

$^1/_2$ c brandy

$^1/_2$ c honey

3 oz honey roasted nuts

3 Tbl olive oil

3 Tbl brown sugar

1 Tbl chopped summer savory

1 Tbl cornstarch

1 clove chopped garlic

Brown chicken well in olive oil. While chicken is browning, combine honey, brandy and brown sugar, stirring until sugar is dissolved. When chicken is browned, add nuts and brandy mixture; reduce heat to a simmer when this mixture begins to boil. Cover and simmer for fifteen minutes. Mix cornstarch with water until dissolved. Remove chicken from pan and add cornstarch mixture, stirring until this mixture begins to thicken, and remove from heat. Serve over wild rice.

Serves 4.

Spare Tire Enchiladas

A friend of mine had a flock of chickens and several roosters. One of the roosters, "George," was particularly exuberant about his male prowess. He would attack people gathering eggs, other roosters, dogs, and one day he attacked his owner once too often. Needless to say, George was quickly dispatched to "Universal Wonderment". That left the problem of what to do with the mortal remains of poor ol' George. Thinking (probably a little too quickly), I decided we should kill the same bird twice with one rock and make enchiladas. Even though we boiled him until he fell off his bones, George still got the last laugh. He was tasty, but it was like chewing on a piece of old tire. By using a decent, mild mannered chicken, you will be relieved of George's rubberized effect.

1 large onion
3 cloves garlic
3 to 5 lb chicken
1 tsp salt
4 Tbl red chili powder
27 oz can chopped green chili
2 Tbl lard or butter
2 Tbl flour
7 oz grated longhorn cheese
12 corn tortillas

Dice onion and slice garlic into thin slivers. Place chicken, onion, garlic and salt into a large pot, cover with water; bring to a boil. Cover and continue boiling until meat begins to fall off the bones. Turn off heat and remove from broth. After chicken has cooled, remove meat from bones. Add red chili to 2 cups broth. Preheat oven to 325. Melt lard or butter in a skillet, and remove 2 cups broth and add red chili to broth, stirring until powder is dissolved. Brown flour and stir in chili broth, removing from heat when mixture begins to thicken. Layer the bottom of a 12"x14" cake pan with tortillas. Add a layer of chicken, then a layer of green chili. Pour $1/2$ of the red chili over the top, topping this layer with cheese. Repeat this until chicken, chili and cheese are gone. Bake at 325 for 25 minutes. Wrap the remaining tortillas in aluminum foil, and place in oven for the last ten minutes.

Serves 4

Ma's Drunken Chicken

Ma didn't want Dad to get drunk, so she used the wine on the chicken...

$^1/_4$ lb butter
12 chicken breasts or thighs
1 large bell pepper
1 medium onion
8 oz mushrooms
24 oz Chablis

Melt butter in a large skillet on medium heat and brown chicken. While chicken is browning, chop vegetables into bite sized pieces. When chicken is browned, add vegetables and wine. Simmer for twenty to twenty-five minutes. Serve over rice or noodles. This meal takes only 30 to 35 minutes to prepare.

Serves 4.

Italian Baked Chicken

Some of the best ideas come from not knowing what to do with
what you have on hand. I had salad dressing, but nothing to make
salad with, and a chicken but nothing to stuff it with. However I had
my trusty syringe and here are the results.

8 oz bottle Italian salad dressing
2 $^1/_2$ to 3 lb baking chicken
4 oz finely chopped celery
4 oz finely chopped mushrooms

Preheat oven to 350. Strain dressing through a wire strainer, saving
the herbs and spices. **(Look at Shrimp Vermicelli on page 110 to
find a use for the herbs and spices.)** Inject the entire liquid portion
of the dressing into the chicken. Stuff chicken with celery and mushrooms. Cover with aluminum foil and bake at 350 for 55 minutes,
or until the legs pull off easily, removing the foil after 30 minutes to
allow the bird to brown.

Serves 2.

Frenchy's Barbecued Chicken

Necessity may be the mother of invention, but cowboys are the fathers of invention, of which this recipe is a prime example. Having chicken to barbecue, but no sauce, and being too lazy to make the sixty mile trip to town was the inspiration for this dish.

12 pieces chicken legs or thighs
8 oz bottle French salad dressing

Inject chicken thoroughly. Cook over open coals or on a gas grill for twenty minutes, turning every five minutes.

Serves 4.

Blue Lake Chicken

Originally prepared in a cabin nestled under the pines next to Blue Lake, in the high Sierra mountains, this is a favorite of rooster wranglers everywhere.

12 chicken breasts or thighs
8 oz white Worcestershire sauce
10 oz vermicelli
1 finely chopped medium onion
2 cloves grated garlic
8 oz mushrooms
6 oz chopped black olives
1 tsp sweet basil
1 tsp thyme
1Tbl chopped fresh parsley
6 oz Chablis
$^1/_2$ pt cream
8 oz sour cream

Preheat oven to 325. Inject chicken with Worcestershire sauce. Brown in butter and bake at 325 for twenty minutes. While chicken is baking, prepare vermicelli according to package instructions. Sauté vegetables and spices in butter remaining from browning chicken until onions are clear. Add the Chablis to this and immediately add cream and sour cream, stirring constantly until mixture begins to boil. Remove from heat. Drain vermicelli and place into a 8" x12" cake pan. Pour half the sauce over this, top with chicken and pour the remaining sauce over the chicken.

Serves 4.

Santa Fe Kiev

You don't live in New Mexico for long without becoming addicted to chili. Sometimes it seems as though nothing tastes right unless it has chili in it. Therefore, while working on a ranch near Santa Fe, the chili accidentally wound up in the Kiev.

4 Tbl butter
1 Tbl minced onion
1 clove minced garlic
1 Tbl diced green chili
4 boneless chicken breasts
2 oz cream cheese

Melt butter over low heat, then sauté onion, garlic and green chili until clear and remove from heat. Using a meat mallet, pound bone side of breasts until they are flat. After flattening breast, spoon equal amounts of sautéed ingredients, reserving 2 Tbl of butter mixture. Place $^1/_2$ tsp cream cheese on each breast, roll and secure with toothpicks, and place into a pie pan. Pour remaining butter mixture over the breasts, cover and refrigerate eight to twenty-four hours. Bake at 350 for 20 minutes.

Serves 2.

Black Bart's Chicken Caper

Black Bart was a famous stagecoach bandit of the California gold rush days. Playing poker and dining with members of the San Francisco Police department he would discover when large quantities of gold were to be shipped. For several years he carried on with his double life, that of a friend of law officers, and that of bandit without injury to himself, or his victims. Finally he met with justice when a shotgun rider killed him. It was a surprise to everyone when the flour sack he wore over his head during robberies was removed, for he had been totally unsuspected in the robberies.

2 Tbl olive oil
1 $^1/_2$ lb boneless chicken breast
juice from 1 lemon
1 small onion
1 tsp capers
1 tsp Italian seasoning
$^1/_4$ tsp garlic powder
12 oz beer

Brown chicken in olive oil. Mince onion. When chicken is browned add remaining ingredients and simmer for twenty minutes.

Serves 4.

Prairie Chicken

Had a real bad experience on the prairies of Nebraska one day. Was riding a real rank horse that decided if a cow could jump over the moon, he could jump over the chicken house. Needless to say, we did not quite make it, and as it was before sunrise, all of those poor birds were trapped. We salvaged what we could and ate the rest. (The one legged hebecame the best layer, although we never could get her in a chicken house again.)

5 Tbl butter
9 chicken drumsticks
$^1/_2$ c minced onion
$^1/_2$ c minced bell pepper
2 large cloves chopped garlic
2 Tbl concentrated lemon juice
1 c Chablis

Melt butter in skillet. Brown chicken in butter, add remaining ingredients. Cover and simmer for 25 minutes. Serve over rice or pasta.

Serves 3.

Mountain Valley Chicken

There must be some sort of genetic defect among chickens, or maybe chicken farmers trying to jump over the hen house. Has to be one or the other, or why else would you buy so many packages of chicken legs or thighs with odd numbers of limbs when chickens have two legs?

9 chicken legs or thighs
$^1/_2$ lb butter
5 Tbl Chablis
5 Tbl sour cream
$^1/_2$ tsp garlic powder
$^1/_2$ tsp seasoning salt

Combine all ingredients except chicken in a saucepan and sauté over low heat until butter and sour cream are melted. Inject sauce evenly into chicken and broil or grill ten minutes on each side.

Serves 3.

Lamb

The American Rancher's contribution to the wolf re-population effort

Rocky Mountain Lamb

This tasty lamb dish was "brewed" in the high Rocky Mountains of Colorado. Using Coors is not an absolute must. However it is in keeping with the spirit of the recipe.

1 ½ lb lamb chops
12 oz beer
½ c water
2 Tbl olive oil
¼ c capers
¼ tsp garlic juice
¼ tsp onion juice
1 tsp cornstarch

Brown lamb in olive oil. Add remaining ingredients, reserving water and cornstarch. Simmer for 15 minutes. After meat has simmered, remove meat from broth. Combine water and cornstarch, stirring until smooth. Bring broth to a boil and stir in cornstarch. Continue stirring until mixture thickens. Serve over pasta.

Serves 2.

Irish Leg O' Lamb

You don't have to be Irish to appreciate this delicacy, deep basted with Bailey's Irish Cream. This recipe is dedicated to my Irish ancestors.

5 - 6 lb leg of lamb
2 cloves garlic
½ c Bailey's Irish Cream
¼ c Orange Curacao
6 Tbl brown sugar
1 tsp mint extract

Preheat oven to 300. Brown roast. Slice garlic in half lengthwise, make 4 slices in leg and insert garlic. Inject liquor evenly into leg. Bake at 300 for 3 hours. When roast is done, combine Orange Curacao, mint extract and brown sugar, mixing well. Pour this mixture evenly over the lamb and light with a match. Serve after flame dies.

Serves 6.

English Bedded Lamb

This delicious meal is what my Irish ancestors fed my English ancestors the day after having leg of lamb, which is probably why I have
both Irish and English blood in my veins.

4 c diced Irish Leg O' Lamb
11 ½ oz can vegetable juice
8 oz button mushrooms
8 oz fettuccine
1 small onion
1 bell pepper
2 stalks celery
2 Tbl olive oil
½ tsp dried crushed basil
½ tsp garlic salt

Cook fettuccine as per package instructions. Dice all vegetables. Sauté
onion and mushrooms until clear then add lamb, bell pepper, celery,
garlic salt, basil and vegetable juice. Bring to a boil, then reduce to a
simmer for 10 minutes and serve over fettuccine.

Serves 4.

Irish Orange Chops

Another of my ancestors' recipes. It seems as though the Irish women were always trying to find a way to dispose of the liquor before the men found it. Cooking with it was always the most popular with my mother's side of the family.

4 center cut lamb chops
½ c Bailey's Irish Cream
½ c orange curacao
2 Tbl olive oil
2 Tbl un-roasted peanuts
1 Tbl summer savory

Brown lamb and peanuts in olive oil. Add liquor, cover and simmer for 15 to 20 minutes, or until liquor is nearly evaporated. Serve on a bed of wild rice.

Serves 2.

Dry Gulch Lamb

I once started a simple little project which bushwhacked me better than an Apache in a dry gulch. It started out as a simple matter of replacing the clutch in my pickup. Of course anything which combines me with grease always seems to take more than one try. The first time took me nearly three days, while the fifth time took me a little less than three hours. The experience gave me a whole new appreciation of mechanics.

4 shoulder lamb chops
3 Tbl olive oil
4 oz fresh mushrooms
1 bell pepper
2 cloves garlic
4 oz crushed or slivered almonds
1 tsp dried crushed cilantro
1 tsp rosemary
½ tsp salt
10 oz sherry

Brown lamb in olive oil and remove from heat. Slice mushrooms in half, chop onions and bell pepper. Slice garlic into small slivers. Add all ingredients to lamb, cover and refrigerate 24 hours. Remove from refrigerator, simmer while covered for 20 minutes. Serve on a bed of rice.

Serves 2.

San Pedro Parks Lamb

This was the culmination of attempting to haul three horses to San Pedro Parks Wilderness in New Mexico. After having to unload the horses twice because the road was several degrees steeper than my truck could handle, we were told that the next hill was even steeper. After setting up camp in the dark, I prepared this dish under a sky filled with stars, softly silhouetting the mountains, with the only noises being the crackle of the fire, the hooting of an owl, the occasional snort of a horse and the bugle of a bull elk.

2 Tbl olive oil
4 large lamb chops
1 medium onion
16 oz can peeled tomatoes
7 oz can whole green chili

Brown lamb in olive oil. Peel and chop onion. Add onion, chili and tomatoes to lamb. Cover and simmer for twenty minutes.

Serves 2.

Yukon Lamb

Up in the Yukon it is reputed to get so cold you need to add anti-freeze to keep it from freezing your food while it is cooking. This dish will keep your food and you from freezing!

4 lamb shoulder chops
2 Tbl butter
1 tsp garlic salt
6 whole cloves
2 oz almond slivers
6 oz frozen orange juice concentrate
6 oz water
1 oz Yukon Jack Bourbon (may be substituted with Southern Comfort)
1 tsp peppermint extract
2 Tbl cornstarch
12 oz evaporated milk

Brown chops in butter. When chops are browned on both sides, sprinkle garlic salt, cloves and almond slivers evenly over them. Pour orange juice, water, bourbon and mint extract over this. Cover and simmer twenty minutes. Remove meat from pan. Blend cornstarch with evaporated milk until smooth. Add to broth in pan, stirring until mixture thickens. Serve over noodles or rice.

Serves 4.

Rosemary Lamb

Handed down from an old Basque sheepherder this is an elegant, yet simple dish to prepare.

4 lamb chops
1C chopped Portabella mushrooms
½ C heavy cream
¼ C Port wine
2T Olive oil
2 cloves garlic
2 green onions
1 tsp fresh rosemary

Pre heat olive oil on medium heat. While oil is heating, chop garlic and onion. When oil is hot, add garlic, onion, rosemary and lamb. Cook each side of chops two minutes (or until medium rare). Remove chops, and put portabellas in skillet. Add Port, stirring until wine is evaporated. Add cream and bring to a boil, stirring constantly. Once cream is boiling, reduce to a simmer, stirring occasionally until cream thickens. Pour cream sauce over chops and serve.

Serves 2.

Seafood

Cowboys and Fishermen never Lie

(But their truth may be "slightly" distorted...)

Alaskan Pepper Shrimp

I discovered this genuine Eskimo dish while working for the government. It seems there were too many moose in Alaska, so the government contracted me to drive the excess moose into Canada, as they did not have their green cards.

8 oz fresh peeled shrimp
8 oz extra fine egg noodles
¼ C water
½ green bell pepper
½ red bell pepper
¼ tsp horseradish powder
½ tsp crushed hot chili pepper

Cook noodles as per package instructions. While noodles are cooking, chop bell peppers. Place water and shrimp into a sauce pan on high. Sprinkle shrimp with horseradish and pepper; stir until shrimp are pink and remove from heat. Drain shrimp and noodles. Combine all ingredients and serve.

Serves 2.

Sioux City Scallops

This is a recipe I acquired from a friend of mine in Sioux City Iowa. Half Indian and Half Italian, Luiege Big Bull is a magician with seafood!

16 oz pkg fettuccine
1 lb scallops
8 oz sliced mushrooms
2 large cloves garlic
¾ c chardonnay
3 Tbl butter
¼ c scallions
4 fresh basil leaves
¼ tsp black pepper

Cook fettuccine as per package instructions.

While water is heating cut garlic into slivers, chop scallions and basil leaves into small pieces. Just before adding pasta to water, melt butter over medium heat in a covered skillet. When butter is melted, add mushrooms, scallions, garlic, basil and pepper. Sauté this mixture for 2 to 3 minutes, stirring occasionally. Add scallops and chardonnay; when this mixture begins to boil reduce to a slow simmer, cover and cook for twelve minutes. (Placing fettuccine into boiling water immediately after covering scallops will time everything to finish at the same time.) Serve scallops over fettuccine.

Serves 4.

Virginia City Cod

This recipe was developed during a break between the camel and ostrich races at Virginia City, Nevada. It was kind of a wild weekend, and we weren't sure where the cod came from, but it worked.

1 lb cod fillets
½ bell pepper
1 carrot
6 Tbl white Worcestershire sauce
2 Tbl butter

Preheat oven to 350. Chop bell pepper and carrot into fine pieces, and sauté in butter until pepper is clear. Place fish into a 9" pie pan, and cover with bell pepper and carrot. Pour Worcestershire sauce over this and bake for fifteen minutes at 350.

Serves 2.

"Save a cow...eat a fish!"

Great White Revenge

Roping buffalo on the Australian coast is a little more dangerous than roping bulls here in the States. Once I roped a big bull which weighed close to a ton, got dallied up, then didn't have any place to tie him to. Since he outweighed my horse by a thousand pounds, I just had to kind of go where he took me so my horse wouldn't get pulled over or lose my rope. Since we were right next to the ocean, he thought he would take a swim to cool off and possibly drown me in the process. Luckily I use a fifty foot rope and was able to pitch him enough slack so he could tire himself swimming, as my horse's feet weren't even getting wet. Just as I was starting to pull him back in there was a tremendous explosion of water. It was plain to see that a Great White shark was attacking MY bull. After taking two hits, the head was all that was left of that poor ol' bull, and the shark was coming back for that! Well, when the shark bit down on that head, I kicked old Paint into a high lope and hooked that shark as neatly as a toad shucks a fly from the air. Once I had him beached, I realized it was way past lunch, and I was a long way from home, so this is what I made out of that buffalo bull stealing shark.

3 six ounce shark fillets (Not necessarily Great White)
12 oz cream
¼ lb butter
4 oz mushrooms
½ c chopped celery
1 small onion
3 eggs
$1/3$ c Chablis
1 tsp tarragon
1 Tbl cornstarch

Soak shark in cream 6 to 8 hours. When shark is ready to be cooked, preheat oven to 350. Separate eggs and beat whites until stiff. Remove fillets from cream, dip in the egg whites and place in a shallow baking dish. Spread the remaining whites evenly over fillets and bake at 350 for twenty minutes. While shark is cooking, chop onion finely and slice mushrooms. Combine vegetables, tarragon, sautéing them in butter until clear. Add the cream from marinating the shark, reserving $^1/_2$ c, and the wine.

Beat the egg yolks and add them to this mixture; slowly heat to a simmer. Blend the cornstarch with reserved cream until smooth and stir into sauce. Continue stirring until mixture starts to thicken, and remove from heat. When shark is done serve with sauce poured over the top. Remaining sauce may be served over your choice of rice or pasta.

Serves 4.

Klondike Soufflé

This would undoubtedly be tastier if it were made with freshly caught salmon cooked in a camp along the banks of the Yukon River. Since it takes so much trouble to get there from Arizona, and because of the rarity of catching a salmon big enough to eat out of a watering trough, canned salmon and imagination had to do.

15 ½ oz can salmon
8 oz cream cheese
6 eggs
4 oz fresh mushrooms
$1/_2$ pt whipping cream
$1/_4$ lb butter
$1/_3$ c flour
1 tsp garlic powder
1 tsp cayenne pepper
$1/_2$ tsp salt
$1/_2$ tsp baking powder

Preheat oven to 400. Melt butter in a sauce pan over low heat. While butter is melting, finely chop mushrooms. Combine mushrooms with salt, garlic powder and cayenne pepper. Sauté this for two minutes in butter and remove from heat. Melt cream cheese in a microwave or double boiler. While cheese is melting, separate eggs and beat whites until stiff, then whip the cream until stiff. When cheese has melted, combine all ingredients EXCEPT egg whites and cream. Mix until well blended. Fold in egg whites and cream until thoroughly mixed. Pour this into a bread pan and bake for twenty minutes at 400.

Serves 4.

Wagon Wheel Quiche

I was hauling a wagon load of dudes back to the lodge on a breakfast ride one day, when a bull moose spooked the team. Needless to say the team ran hell bent for leather towards home, taking all the strength I had to get them slowed back down to a walk within a half mile. No sooner did I get them back to a walk, did one of the wagon's back wheels come off, spooking the team once more. Luckily, this time I got them stopped in about fifty feet, and no one was hurt. It was an experience that those tourists, as well as myself, will never forget.

9 inch pie shell (see page 127)
$^1/_2$ lb scallops
4 oz herb and garlic soft cream cheese
(If not available blend $^1/_2$ tsp garlic powder, $^1/_2$ tsp Italian seasoning, $^1/_2$ tsp summer savory and $^1/_4$ tsp dill into the cream cheese)
3 eggs
$^1/_2$ pt cream
$^1/_2$ c flour
Preheat oven to 410. Distribute scallops evenly across bottom of pie shell. Melt cream cheese in a microwave or double boiler. While cheese is melting separate eggs and whip whites until stiff, beat yolks until frothy. Whip cream until stiff. Fold egg whites and cream together, then add yolks. Mix in flour gradually, then add cream cheese mixing slowly until ingredients are thoroughly mixed. Pour batter into pie shell and bake 35 minutes or until a knife inserted into the middle comes out clean.

Serves 4.

Combinations

For those times when you have "nothing to cook."

Fettuccine Tremintina

This recipe was developed on the 4V ranch, just outside of the metropolis of Tremintina, New Mexico. Tremintina is so large that even the Post Master's address is general delivery.

16 oz package fettuccine
½ lb hot Italian sausage
½ lb sweet Italian sausage
½ lb grated provolone cheese
7.5 oz tomato puree
1 med onion
1 large clove garlic
2 tsp Italian seasoning
Preheat oven to 350.
Cut sausage into bite sized pieces. Chop onion and garlic finely. Brown sausage together with onion and garlic. While meat is browning, cook pasta, cutting 2 minutes from cooking time recommended on package. When sausage and pasta are done, mix Italian seasoning with tomato puree. Place $1/_3$ pasta in the bottom of a casserole dish. Top this with one third of the sausage mixture, then $1/_3$ of the tomato puree and finally $1/_3$ of the provolone cheese. Repeat these layers 2 more times, cover and bake at 350 for 25 minutes.

Serves 4.

Bork Stew

No, this is not a favorite of the judge, but it will be if he ever tries it. "Bork" is the result of genetic research in the kitchen, half beef, half pork - all delicious.

1 gallon water
2 lb beef stew meat
2 lb pork stew meat
10 freshly roasted and peeled green chilies
6 potatoes
2 white onions
2 cloves garlic
3 tsp summer savory
1 $1/_2$ tsp salt
1 tsp peppercorns
1 tsp sweet basil

Brown meat in a large dutch oven. While meat is browning, wash and cut potatoes into bite sized pieces, peel and chop onion and garlic. When meat is browned, add remaining ingredients, cover and cook over medium heat for 4 hours.

Serves 8 to 10.

Surf In Turf

While in a restaurant one day I noticed an item called Surf n' Turf.
Being the curious type, I ordered it and received steak and crab. The
meal was delicious, but if you want the flavors of both beef and seafood, why go to the trouble of having the extra dishes to wash from
cooking both separately?

5 lb rump roast
2 large haddock, halibut or cod fillets
1 c white Zinfandel
2 Tbl butter
¼ c minced onion
¼ c cream or half & half
2 cloves minced garlic
1 tsp chopped cilantro
1 egg yolk
3' cotton twine

Preheat oven to 300. Combine all ingredients EXCEPT roast, fish
and egg yolk into a small saucepan. Heat slowly over low heat, stirring occasionally until butter is melted. While butter is melting, slice
roast lengthwise into thirds. When butter is melted, remove from heat
and blend in egg yolk. When sauce is blended, place a fillet on the
bottom third of roast and spread one third of the sauce over the top.
Place the middle third of the roast on top of this and the second fillet, spreading $^1/_2$ of the remaining sauce. Cover this with the remaining third of roast and bind with cotton twine. Spread remaining sauce
over the meat and roast at 300 for two hours.

Serves 6.

Ma's Stolen Taco Meat

This is a recipe given to my mother from a small restaurant in Beaumont, California. Everyone who has ever tried it is in agreement that this is the most mouth watering, delicious taco meat they have ever eaten. (I will soon be in court with Ma for stealing this one!)

1 lb beef stew meat
1 lb pork stew meat
1 lb lamb stew meat

CAUTION: Do not substitute any of the above meats with hamburger as a quicker cooking time does not allow the flavors to properly blend!

24 oz can green chili sauce
24 oz can red chili sauce

Brown all meat. Drain and place all ingredients in a slow cooker for eight hours. Drain off liquid and place meat in your favorite type of taco shell; garnish to your preference and enjoy the best taco you have ever eaten.

Makes approximately 30 tacos.

Coyote Goulash

In Montana, one of the winter activities is hunting coyotes, who not only cost some ranchers thousands of dollars in lost livestock, but whose pelts, in a good year can bring as much as $250 apiece. With the invention of the snowmobile, hunting these critters has become sort of a dual sport. To test your abilities for flying a sled, you chase a "yote", getting as close to it as possible. To test your shooting ability, you then stop the sled, unsling your rifle and attempt to shoot the yote which is running away from you as fast as thirty five or forty miles an hour. Not many yotes are taken in this manner, but you surely get an adrenaline rush trying. This recipe is dedicated to Rex (I'm sure he wants his last name to remain anonymous). It seems Rex was spending an enjoyable outing with his parents when he spotted a yote. Since he was in a large clearing, he was up to sixty miles an hour and on his quarry instantly. The only problem was that the yote jumped on the sled with him. Needless to say, Rex made a hasty retreat, the yote learned to drive a snowmobile, and Rex's parents had a ball telling everyone in Wilsall of Rex's encounter.

½ lb boneless chicken breast

½ lb beef cube steak

¼ lb smoked ham

8 oz cream cheese
8 oz sour cream
5 oz sliced Spanish olives
5 oz Chablis
4 oz diced green chili
5 green onions
2 Tbl butter

Cut chicken, beef and ham into bite sized pieces and brown in butter. While meat is browning, drain olives and chop onion. When meat is browned, add remaining ingredients, bring to a boil, and then reduce to a simmer. Cover and simmer for 20 minutes. Serve over rice, noodles, corn tortillas or toast.

Serves 4.   *87*

Sierra Sheep Camp Goulash

I was checking on some sheep in Donner Pass in the Sierra Nevada Mountains when I concocted this recipe. The original name was Donner Pass Goulash, until a friend pointed out that the name might have an impact on the dish due to the historical maladies associated with the area.

1 ½ lb lamb hamburger
½ lb bacon
12 oz sherry
10 oz pkg egg noodles
1 medium onion
1 clove garlic
½ pt cream
1 tsp dried crushed cilantro
1 tsp salt
2 Tbl cornstarch

Cook noodles as per package instructions. Cut bacon into one inch strips and cook until crisp; drain and place into one quart saucepan. Brown lamb, drain and add to bacon. While bacon and lamb are cooking, chop garlic and onion, then stir into meat. Add remaining ingredients, reserving cream and cornstarch. Simmer for twenty minutes. Blend cornstarch into cream and stir into meat mixture, stirring constantly until mixture begins to thicken. Serve over noodles.

Serves 4.

Superstition Chile

This recipe is dedicated to the memory of the "Lost Dutchman", whose legendary mine still lies hidden somewhere in the deceiving beauty of Arizona's Superstition Mountains.

1 lb pinto beans
½ lb beef stew meat
½ lb pork stew meat
½ lb lamb stew meat
24 oz can red chili sauce
24 oz can green chili sauce.

Wash and soak beans overnight. Brown meat and place all ingredients into an eight quart slow cooker on low for eight to ten hours.

Serves 6 to 8.

Champagne Stew

The older you get the better your chances of making it to the "'til death do part" bit. This recipe was first concocted for a good friend's fifth wedding. In his late sixties he did quite well not only in acquiring a young bride but also in having a built in nurse which relieved his daughter from the task of mending him after his horse wrecks...

1 liter dry champagne
1 - 2 lb pork shoulder roast
1 lb polish sausage
1 lb lamb stew meat
1 lb uncooked jumbo macaroni shells
1 lb peeled baby carrots
1 head red cabbage
1 large onion
1 bunch celery
2 - 7 ¾ oz cans hot style tomato sauce
1 Tbl garlic salt

Cut meat into bite sized pieces and brown in a dutch oven. While meat is browning cut vegetables in bite
sized pieces. When meat is browned, add remaining ingredients, reserving macaroni shells. Bring stew to a boil, then reduce to a simmer for three hours, stirring occasionally. Add macaroni shells during last twenty minutes of cooking, making certain that shells are completely immersed in stew.

Serves 12. Leftovers may be frozen.

Rio Grande Stuffed Steak

This recipe originally contained crawfish caught in the Rio Grande River, near Socorro, New Mexico. Since it is easier for most people to acquire shrimp, they are used here in place of the crawfish.

2 - 8 oz round tip steaks
6 fresh jumbo shrimp
2 green onions
1 clove garlic
1 medium lemon
1Tbl sesame oil
$\frac{1}{2}$ pt cream
$\frac{1}{4}$ c Chablis
$\frac{1}{2}$ tsp cayenne pepper
1 tsp dried chopped cilantro
1 tsp honey
$\frac{1}{2}$ tsp salt
2 Tbl cornstarch

Preheat oven to 350. Dice onion and garlic. Squeeze juice out of $\frac{1}{2}$ of the lemon. Sauté onion and garlic in sesame oil until clear. Add $\frac{1}{2}$ cup cream, Chablis, pepper, cilantro, honey, lemon juice and salt. Bring to a low boil, stirring constantly. Remove from heat when mixture begins to boil. Shell and clean shrimp. Place three shrimp on each steak. Spoon 1 tsp of sauce on each shrimp. Roll steaks and secure with toothpicks. Slice other half of lemon, placing the slices on top of the steaks. Top each steak with I tsp of sauce. Bake for twenty minutes at 350. When steaks have been baking for eighteen minutes, place the remaining sauce over medium heat. Blend cornstarch with remaining cream and stir into sauce. Continue stirring until sauce thickens and remove from heat. Pour sauce over steaks and serve.

Serves 2

Vegetables

So good even the kids will eat them

Casa De Blanco   Concordia Ranch

Triple Diamond Veggie Rolls

The Triple Diamond Ranch is located just outside
of Timbuck Three, which is approximately five hundred miles north-
east of Timbuck Two. Working here can be hazardous to your health.
The cattle are Longhorn crossed with buffalo, and a little
Rocky Mountain Sheep thrown in to assure they won't fall off the
mountains, which are so steep they make the Matterhorn look like the
foothills to the Great Plains. Instead of riding horses, you ride
Muoats, which are mules crossed with mountain goats. Muoats are
the only rideable animals able to traverse the Triple Diamond without
requiring the
rider to wear a parachute.

1 package crescent roll dough
8 spears broccoli
8 florets cauliflower
4 spinach leaves
8 tsp tomato sauce
2 tsp garlic salt
2 tsp oregano powder
2 tsp cream cheese
4 tsp grated cheddar cheese

Preheat oven to 375. Separate rolls into individual
triangles, stretching each one until it is almost
ready to pull apart. Wash the vegetables. Place one
half leaf spinach lengthwise on each triangle of
dough. Place one spear of broccoli and one floret
of cauliflower on the wide end of each triangle.
Sprinkle 1/4 tsp of oregano and 1/4 tsp garlic salt
and top with 1 tsp tomato sauce. Place 1/4 tsp
cream cheese and 1/4 tsp cheddar cheese on each
triangle, roll and place on an un-greased cookie
sheet. Bake at 375 for twelve to fifteen minutes, or
until golden brown.

Serves 4.

Rosemary Garlic Mashed Potatoes

Why have the same old mashed potatoes all of the time? This elegant twist turns everyday 'taters into a treat!

4 large potatoes
4 large cloves garlic
1/8 c fresh Rosemary leaves
4 oz cream cheese

Peel potatoes and cut into 1/2 inch pieces. Smash garlic cloves and peel. Place potatoes, garlic and rosemary into a pot, cover with water and boil for 10 minutes or until potatoes are soft. Drain, add cream cheese and mash.

Serves 4.

El Paso Quiche

You can always count on getting low on groceries when you don't get to town at the end of the month. On this occasion I had more flats than spares and had to wait for a couple of repair kits to be delivered from Santa Fe.

9" pie shell (seee page 127)
7 oz can green chili sauce
1/2 pt cream
4 eggs
1/2 c flour
4 oz grated cheddar cheese
1/4 tsp salt

Preheat oven to 375. Whip cream until stiff. Separate eggs and beat whites until stiff. Mix egg yolks with chili sauce, salt. Gently fold cream and egg whites together. Next fold chili mixture with egg and cream mixture, then slowly mix in flour until all ingredients are well blended. Pour this mixture into pie shell and bake at 375 for 30 to 35 minutes or until a knife inserted into the middle comes out clean.

Serves 4.

Enchanted Beans

Legend has it that a northern New Mexico sorceress would make these beans to steal horses . Their aroma would attract cowboys from miles around (even against the wind). Once a cowboy would eat the beans he would immediately get the urge to take a siesta. Upon awaking the hapless cowboy would find himself afoot as the sorceress was would make off with their horses as they napped.

1 lb kidney beans
1 lb white navy beans
½ lb chopped ham
1 bunch finely sliced celery
1 bell pepper, finely chopped
6 cups chicken broth
2 Tbl red chili powder
2 Tbl mustard powder

Combine all ingredients in a slow cooker on low for 6 hours or on high for 4 hours.

Serves 4.

Camouflaged Squash

Use this one and the kids won't even know they are eating their vegetables!

1 small spaghetti squash
1 lb Italian sausage
16 oz can diced tomatoes
1 tsp Italian seasoning.

Preheat oven to 350. Slice squash lengthwise and remove seeds. Bake face down for 45 minutes. While squash is cooking, slice sausage into one inch pieces and cook until done. When squash is done, remove strands of squash with a fork into a mixing bowl. Combine all ingredients and mix well.

Serves 4.

Zucchini

It took me several dictionaries to find zucchini. Just out of curiosity it would be interesting to know how and why it acquired it's spelling. My mother used to tell me if I did not know how to spell a word to look it up in the dictionary. I kept looking for zucchini under the S's and couldn't figure out why it wasn't there.

1 medium zucchini
1 c water
1 tsp oregano
$^1/_2$ tsp garlic powder
$^1/_2$ tsp sweet basil
Slice zucchini into inch slices. Steam for five minutes over one cup of water containing oregano, garlic powder and sweet basil.

Serves 4.

Spinach Soufflé

Spinach might be good for Popeye, but Olive Oil never could stand it out of a can. This is only one of the ways Popeye ate his spinach at home.

1 c finely chopped spinach
4 oz cream cheese
½ c cream
3 eggs
2 Tbl butter
1 clove garlic
½ tsp salt

Preheat oven to 375. Place butter into an eight inch cake pan and place in oven to melt butter. Place spinach in a large mixing bowl. Place eggs, garlic and salt in a mixing bowl and mix on high for one minute. Slice cream cheese into small pieces, add to the egg mixture and mix on high for two minutes. Combine egg mixture with spinach, stirring slowly by hand until all ingredients are well blended. Remove butter from oven and swirl cake pan to evenly distribute butter, then pour batter into the pan and bake 25 to 30 minutes or until golden brown.

Serves 4.

Texas Lasagna

Texas. It seems like that state produces a whole different breed of people from the rest of the country. They are all shot up with pride about how their state has the biggest and best of everything. The only thing I want to know, if Texas has the biggest and best of everything, why is it that so many Texans leave the state to go hunting and fishing, or to buy cattle and horses? (While claiming that they could have done better by staying in Texas, of course!)

2 tsp Italian seasoning
1 tsp garlic salt
1 lb Ricotta cheese
28 oz can whole green chili
1 large tomato
1 medium zucchini

Preheat oven to 300. Blend Italian seasoning with garlic salt and Ricotta cheese. Drain chili and spread $^1/_2$ evenly over bottom of bread pan. Cover with $^1/_2$ of cheese mixture. Spread remaining chili on top of this, covering with remaining cheese mixture. Bake for 20 minutes at 300.

Serves 4.

Soups Salads & Pasta

Warming up for the main course

Canyon Wall Salad

Following a bunch of cows down a canyon gives a person time to enjoy the scenery, as they usually have nowhere to go but the direction you point them. It was while doing this that I was struck with the idea of a layered salad. The canyon walls were layered in rich colors varying from rich browns to deep reds and light grays, evidence of the ocean which had once covered this spot.

1 lb bacon
1 head lettuce
1 large red onion
1 large tomato
8 oz sour cream
8 oz mayonnaise (may be substituted with yogurt)
8 oz frozen sweet peas
8 oz grated longhorn cheese

Fry bacon until crisp; drain and crumble. While bacon is frying, shred lettuce, dice onion and slice tomato thinly. Blend sour cream with mayonnaise and diced onion. Build the salad in a large mixing bowl by placing ½ of the lettuce in the bottom, followed by ½ of the bacon, ½ of the peas covered with a layer of tomato slices. Cover this with a layer of dressing and a layer of cheese. Repeat this procedure, cover and refrigerate 4 to 8 hours.

Serves 8.

Layered Italian Salad

As a boy I helped out on farms and ranches around my parents' place in northern California. Most of the people owning these places were of Italian descent and would make their own salami, which was delicious by itself or in a salad. This salad was inspired by these neighbors, and by a beautiful lady who challenged me to make a low-fat salad dressing for it.

16 oz plain yogurt
1 tsp garlic powder
2 Tbl minced onion
2 Tbl mayonnaise
½ tsp sweet basil
½ tsp oregano
(Combine the above ingredients in a bowl and mix thoroughly.)
1 head iceberg lettuce
12 oz dry salami
2 tomatoes
10 oz package frozen peas
6 oz grated romano cheese

Shred the lettuce and chop the salami into bite sized pieces. Slice the tomatoes thinly. In a bowl, place a layer of lettuce then salami, followed by a layer of peas. Cover this with a layer of tomatoes, then dressing and top with a layer of cheese. Repeat these layers, cover and refrigerate 2 to 4 hours.

Serves 4 to 6.

Peachberry Salad

This salad was made from the fruits in one of Johnny Appleseed's orchards. This orchard has the only known peachberry trees in the world. Modern day geneticists have been trying unsuccessfully to duplicate this luscious fruit.

16 oz can sliced cling peaches
1 pt fresh strawberries
2 ¼ oz pkg sliced almonds
4 Tbl cottage cheese
4 Tbl yogurt
1 Tbl sugar in the raw or brown sugar

Clean and slice strawberries. Peel papaya and kiwi, removing seeds from the papaya. Cut fruit into bite sized pieces. Blend sugar and cottage cheese into yogurt. Place fruit into mixing bowl, cover with yogurt mixture and stir until fruit is well covered. Chill and serve.

Serves 4.

Kiwi Salad

Developed on a large Hawaiian ranch, this salad is luscious enough to eat for dessert.

1 Papaya
2 Kiwi
8 oz vanilla yogurt
½ tsp cinnamon

Peel papaya and kiwi, removing seeds from the papaya. Cut fruit into bite sized pieces. Blend cinnamon into yogurt. Place fruit into mixing bowl, cover with yogurt mixture and stir until fruit is well covered. Chill and serve.

Serves 4.

Santa Maria Squash Pasta

A delightful dish developed by Columbus's cook on the Santa Maria to keep the crews happy on the way back to Spain.

8 oz spiral noodles
2 c bite sized pieces of yellow squash
1 med tomato
½ c sherry
1 bay leaf
½ tsp summer savory
¼ tsp garlic powder

Cook pasta as per package instructions. Dice tomato and combine with remaining ingredients. Cover and cook over medium heat for five minutes, stirring occasionally and remove from heat. Drain pasta and combine with squash mixture.

Serves 4.

Capering Chicken Salad

A favorite of Butch Cassidy and the Sundance Kid upon returning
from a robbery run.

Meat from 2 broiled or baked chicken breasts
2 c cooked pasta
2 stalks celery
juice from 1 lime
3 Tbl mayonnaise
2 Tbl pickled sweet red peppers
2 Tbl Dijon mustard
2 tsp capers

Remove Chicken from bone and cut into bite sized pieces. Combine
and mix thoroughly with remaining ingredients. Cover and refrigerate
2 to 4 hours.

Serves 4.

Fourth Of July Potato Salad

This recipe was born in Ireland during the famine and brought to this country by my great grandmother. Her only problem was keeping my great grandfather from stealing the potatoes to make potato mash whiskey.

5 lb potatoes
32 oz jar Miracle Whip
1 doz eggs
1 onion
6 stalks celery
2 large dill pickles
1 Tbl dill weed
$1/_2$ tsp garlic powder

Boil potatoes and let cool to room temperature. While potatoes are cooling hard boil eggs. (To save energy, remove potatoes from water with tongs and boil eggs in the same water.) When eggs and potatoes have cooled, peel and cut into small pieces and place in a large bowl. Peel and dice onion, chop celery and add to eggs and potatoes. Chop pickles and add. Mix remaining ingredients in a separate bowl, then pour over potato mixture and stir until potatoes and eggs are well covered with dressing. Cover and refrigerate four hours.

Serves 10 to 12

Garlic Vermicelli

There is no reason, and no rule which states that you have to be in the kitchen all day to make good food, of which this recipe is a prime example. This is a tasty side dish after spending all day branding, or after a day on the floor of Dow Jones, and it only takes fifteen minutes to prepare!

5 oz vermicelli

5 scallions

$^1/_4$ c Parmesan cheese

$^1/_4$ tsp concentrated garlic juice

Prepare vermicelli according to package instructions. When pasta is done, drain and mix thoroughly with remaining ingredients.
Serves 2.

Shrimp Vermicelli

* To Accompany Italian Baked Chicken on page 58

This side dish was a direct spin-off from Italian Baked Chicken. I didn't have anything to do with the herbs and spices from the Italian dressing, so I used them with shrimp I had just caught out of the stock tank.

10 oz vermicelli
4 oz fresh shrimp
4 oz sliced mushrooms
2 Tbl olive oil
2 Tbl grated parmesan cheese
Herbs and Spices from Italian dressing

Prepare vermicelli as per package instructions. Shell and clean shrimp. Sauté mushrooms, shrimp in olive oil with herbs and spices from Italian Dressing for two minutes. When vermicelli is done, drain and mix with shrimp mixture and cheese.

Serves 4.

Shrimp Lake Salad

A neighbor of mine in Montana had a small lake in one of his pastures which was full of trout, some of which were quite large. After a full day of trying to catch a few for dinner without getting so much as one bite, we concluded that the fish were too full of the fresh water shrimp, which vastly outnumbered the trout, to accept our baited hooks and lures. Following the old adage, "If you can't beat 'em , join 'em," we went home and had shrimp ourselves. This is what we had.

1 lb small cooked, cleaned and de-viened shrimp
1 head lettuce
3 stalks celery
3 green onions
2 c mayonnaise
2 tsp capers
2 tsp white Worcestershire sauce
1 tsp hot mustard powder
1 tsp cayenne pepper
½ tsp salt
½ tsp garlic powder

Clean and chop lettuce, celery and onion. Mix remaining ingredients in a large bowl until well blended. Add vegetables and mix until well covered and shrimp is evenly distributed. Cover and chill for 2 to 3 hours.

Serves 6.

Sun Valley Pasta Salad

Entered the downhill races at Sun Valley one year. Lost real bad. In fact my time was so slow they never bothered to record it because the snow was gone and so was everybody else by the time I finished. This recipe takes a lot less time to prepare than it did for me to finish my race.

6 oz rotini
6 oz jar sweet fried peppers
5 oz jar cocktail onions
2 oz jar pimientos
$^1/_2$ c parmesan cheese

Prepare rotini as per package instructions. When done, drain and mix with remaining ingredients. Chill eight to ten hours.

Serves 4

Dixie Valley Pasta Salad

Dixie Valley lies north of Fallon, Nevada. From the ranch it was 120 miles one way, with the paved road only forty-five miles from the house, so you did not go to town often. Desolate, yet beautiful, and peaceful at night with a full moon glowing on the dry desert peaks surrounding the valley.

16 oz Linguine
8 oz mushrooms
3 oz grated Romano cheese
$1/2$ c chopped parsley
$1/2$ c chopped broccoli
3 green onions
$1/2$ green bell pepper
$1/2$ red bell pepper
$1/4$ tsp garlic powder

Cook pasta as per package directions. While pasta is cooking, chop onion and slice mushrooms, then sauté in butter and garlic powder until onion is clear and remove from heat. When linguine is done, drain and add to onion and mushrooms. Combine all ingredients and mix until pasta and vegetables are coated with cheese.

Serves 6.

Eagles View Pasta Salad

Sitting on top of a mesa, giving my horse a rest after the hard climb up, I happened to look down upon an eagle searching for it's prey. At times gliding, at others hovering in the air as if suspended by invisible twine, it suddenly dove to the ground, snaring an unsuspecting rabbit. It is moments such as these that give a person a chance to see life as provided by nature, and to appreciate the magnitude of creation.

10 oz rotini
6 oz marinated artichoke hearts
4 oz marinated mushrooms
4 oz sliced ripe olives
1/4 c chopped parsley
12 oz Parmesan cheese

Prepare rotini as per package instructions. Drain and mix with remaining ingredients. Chill two to eight hours.

Serves 4.

Poor Man's Stew

This is a New Mexico favorite. Inexpensive to make, this tasty stew is good as either a meal or as an appetizer. It is also guaranteed to warm you up on a cold winter day!

Half gallon water
1lb hamburger
1c chopped green chili
4 potatoes
1 medium onion
4 cloves garlic
1T salt

Peel and chop onion and garlic, then place in a one gallon pot with hamburger on medium heat, until hamburger is browned. While hamburger is browning, peel potatoes and chop into half inch pieces. When hamburger is browned, add remaining ingredients. Turn heat to high until mixture begins to boil. Reduce to a simmer for 20 minutes.

Serves 4.

Fall Gathering Soup

When the aspen leaves turn gold in the fall, it is the signal to move the cattle down out of the mountains before the first snow flies. The work is hard, but enjoyable, especially when you get down to the few animals who refuse to be found. A friend of mine once made the analogy that "its just like hunting elk, only you have to bring them in alive." Since the crews used to gather often number ten or more you need enough to feed a lot of people, and this recipe fits the bill for gathering crews or holiday parties.

7 - 16 oz cans white potatoes
5 lb diced ham
2 large onions
1 gallon milk
1/4 lb butter
5 - 12 oz cans evaporated milk
11/2 lb muenster cheese
1 bunch celery
2 cloves garlic
1 Tbl black pepper
4 bay leaves

Chop onion and sliver garlic into small pieces. Sauté onion and garlic in butter until clear. Chop celery while onion and garlic are sautéing. When onion and garlic are clear, add remaining ingredients, reserving cheese. Cook over medium heat for 35 minutes, stirring every five minutes, making sure soup does not boil. While soup is cooking grate cheese. After soup has been cooking thirty minutes, stir in the cheese and continue cooking until cheese has melted.

Makes approximately two gallons.

Yellowstone Clam Chowder

This hearty chowder, developed after gathering cattle all day along the banks of the Yellowstone River, is guaranteed to both fill and warm you up. As a bonus, it takes less than thirty minutes to prepare.

2 - 14 1/2 oz cans white potatoes
2 - 6 1/2 oz cans clams
9 oz package frozen mixed vegetables
8 oz sliced fresh mushrooms
8 oz cream cheese
1 gallon milk
2 tsp butter
2 stalks celery
3 green onions
1 tsp fresh chopped summer savory
1/4 tsp garlic salt

In a 2 gallon pot, melt butter over medium heat. While butter is melting chop onion, potatoes and celery. When butter is melted, add mushrooms, onion, celery, garlic salt and summer savory. Sauté until onion is clear. Slice cheese and add with remaining ingredients. Simmer, stirring every two to three minutes until cheese is melted.

Makes approximately 2 gallons.

Elko Cream Soup

Fall can be mighty cold at Elko, Nevada. Add to that a wind that makes Chicago's most windy day seem like the eye of a hurricane and you need something to warm you up before you dig into your steak.

4 carrots
4 stalks celery
1 medium onion
32 oz canned white potatoes
2 cloves garlic
1/2 lb butter
1 1/2 lb muenster cheese
1 qt half and half
1 tsp salt
1 tsp white pepper
1/2 tsp horseradish powder

Slice carrots, celery, onion and potatoes. Mince garlic. Sauté carrots, celery, onion, potatoes and garlic in butter until onion is clear, using a one gallon stock pot. Add the remaining ingredients and bring slowly to a simmer, stirring occasionally until cheese is melted.

Serves 8.

Smoky Shrimp Bisque

A perfect start to dinner after spending the day riding the costal ranges of the Pacific Ocean.

20 Med shrimp
10 cloves garlic
1/2 C finely grated Muenster Cheese
1 pt cream
6 cherry tomatoes
3 green onions
2T olive oil
1 t Fresh finely chopped basil
1t fresh, finely chopped Rosemary

Clean and peel shrimp. Peel garlic. Grill garlic and shrimp for 3 minutes (preferably over charcoal,
not gas). Cut cherry tomatoes into fourths. Chop green onion into inch long pieces. Sauté` tomatoes, onion, Basil and Rosemary in olive oil over medium heat for three minutes, stirring occasionally.
Add cream and slowly stir in cheese. Raise heat to medium high. Once cream begins to boil, reduce to a simmer, stirring occasionally until cream begins to thicken. Add shrimp and garlic. Simmer for 2 minutes.

Serves 4.

Deserts

The end is near!

Gravel Road Banana Pie

If nuts are good on a banana split, then why not in a banana pie? This is a question which plagued Socrates, and one which he could not find a chef to adequately answer. After trying this pie, you will find that the answer is that there is no reason.

1-9inch pie crust (page 127)
8 oz cream cheese
6 eggs
½ pt cream
½ c sugar
½ c flour
2 bananas
4 oz walnut pieces

Preheat oven to 375. Melt cream cheese in a microwave or double boiler. While cheese is melting, beat eggs and cream until foamy. When eggs and cream are foamy, slowly add flour, sugar and cream cheese until all ingredients are well mixed. Slice bananas and spread them evenly over the bottom of the pie shell, spreading the nuts evenly over them. Pour the batter into the pie shell and bake at 375 for 30 minutes or until a knife inserted into the middle comes out clean.

Mary's Nut Cake

This is a recipe that was given to my Grandmother by a neighbor. It is a VERY difficult recipe to make. It has been known to fall if taken out of the oven too soon, or if a draft hits it while cooling,but even with it's difficulties, it is worth the effort it takes to build.

8 eggs
8 Tbl sugar
4 Tbl flour
4 Tbl finely chopped walnuts or pecans
1 tsp baking powder
1/2 tsp vanilla

Preheat oven to 350. Separate egg and beat whites
until stiff. Mix and beat all remaining ingredients
until foamy; then GENTLY fold in egg whites.
Pour into two lightly greased and floured cake
pans and cook 30 to 35 minutes.
COOL UPSIDE DOWN, COMPLETELY, IN TINS.

Filling & Frosting For
Mary's Nut Cake

1/2 lb unsalted butter
1/2 c cold coffee
4 beaten eggs
6 Tbl sugar
1/2 c finely ground walnuts or pecans

Mix all ingredients EXCEPT butter and walnuts. Cook over low
heat until it is the consistency of custard. COOL COMPLETELY!!!
When mixture is
completely cool, add butter, mixing until mixture is smooth. Fill and
cover cake, sprinkling ground walnuts on both layers and pressing
them into the sides.

Orange Pecan Pie

Learning the truth of things can often be a funny experience. An Air Force buddy of mine found that out when he went home with me on leave. As would often happen, there would be a bunch of us sitting around drinking beer and swapping stories of what we had done in civilian life. More often than not, whenever I would tell a story, people would laugh and say no such thing ever happened, and Steve would ask me where I came up with such tall tales. When the time came for me to go home on leave, I asked Steve if he would like to go with me and see where these stories came from, to which he readily agreed. On our second day home, we stopped to have a hamburger. Before lunch was served, a friend of mine walked in the door. Instead of giving me a normal greeting to someone he hadn't seen in years, he said, "I'll be damned! You are just the person I've been needing to see! Can you tell me how to gather up six buffalo bulls?" Steve never doubted my stories again.

9" pie crust (see page 127)

¼ lb butter

½ c brown sugar

½ c light corn syrup

½ c dark corn syrup

2 Tbl evaporated milk

2 tsp orange extract

1 tsp vanilla

1½ c pecans

4 eggs

9 inch pie shell

Preheat oven to 350. Combine all ingredients EXCEPT eggs, pecans and pie shell in a saucepan over medium heat, stirring occasionally until butter is melted. Spread pecans evenly over the bottom of the pie shell. Beat eggs until foamy. When butter is melted, blend in the eggs and pour over pecans. Bake at 350 for 50 to 55 minutes or until a knife inserted halfway between the center and edge comes out clean.

Nut Crescents

This is another recipe donated by my mother which is a family favorite. It is a good one to let the kids make as it is almost foolproof. (I say almost, because there is always the chance that somewhere, somehow, and sometimes, even the simplest things may go awry.)

½ cup shorteing
½ c butter
1 ¼ c ground walnuts or almonds
2 c sifted flour
1 Tbl water
1 Tbl vanilla
2 c powdered sugar

Preheat oven to 325. Combine butter and shortening until it attains a creamy texture. Gradually blend in ½ of powdered sugar. Mix in nuts, and then gradually blend in flour. Add vanilla and water and mix well. Using 1 Tbs of dough per cookie, shape into crescents on an ungreased cookie sheet and flatten slightly. Bake for twelve to fifteen minutes at 325. Roll in remaining powdered sugar while still warm.

Cool on cookie racks.

Yule Cake

Some families have forgotten their fruitcake recipe. They just keep sending the same rock-like structure back and forth as the family gag gift. Send this one, and you won't get it back for it will be immediately consumed. This recipe is an old family favorite which I pilfered from my mother. Even people who hate fruitcake like this one.

Preheat oven to 300.

$1 \frac{1}{2}$ c whole Brazil nuts

$1 \frac{1}{2}$ c walnuts

1 c pitted dates

$\frac{1}{2}$ c red maraschino cherries

$\frac{1}{2}$ c green maraschino cherries

$\frac{1}{2}$ c seedless raisins

$\frac{3}{4}$ c sifted flour

$\frac{3}{4}$ c sugar

$\frac{1}{2}$ tsp salt

$\frac{1}{2}$ tsp baking powder

1 tsp vanilla

3 eggs

In a very large bowl, mix nuts and fruit. Combine flour, sugar, salt and baking powder, sift over fruit mixture and mix well. Beat eggs until light and fluffy, add vanilla and blend thoroughly into fruit mixture. Pack into a loaf pan which has been greased and bottom lined with wax paper. Bake at 300 for $1\frac{3}{4}$ to 2 hours, or until firm on top. Cool 10 minutes, loosen edges and turn onto wire rack. Remove wax paper and cool completely. Keep refrigerated.

Pie Crust

Deciding to make a pie (or quiche) after 10 to 14 hours in the saddle, one tends to take as many shortcuts as possible. If you decide to make your own pie crust, the following recipe is about as good as you can get. However you need to be aware that a home made crust will take a little longer to cook as it is usually slightly thicker. Another factor in cooking time will be whether or not you use a metal pie pan or a glass pie dish. Generally, add 10 to 15 minutes the time in the recipes for metal and 15 to 20 minutes for glass.

$^2/_3$ C butter

2 C flour

1 t salt

5 to 6 T ice water

Chill a large mixing bowl in freezer for 5 to 10 minutes. Sift flour into bowl. Cut butter into slivers then cut into flour using a pastry cutter or fork until particles are the size of small peas. Sprinkle with ice water until flour is moist. Divide dough into 2 balls. Lightly dust board or pastry cloth with flour. Roll pastry to about $^1/_8$ inch thick (2" larger than pie tin).

About The Author

Bob Kinford's mother began teaching him to cook before he was five, telling him "You may not always have someone to cook for you." That was one of her premonitions that came true. For much of his adult life Bob has lived alone on remote ranches, cooking for himself and for crew that would come in to help work cattle.

One of the stereotypes of the Cowboy is that they only eat beef, biscuits and beans. Raised in farm and ranch country of Amador County in northern California. Most of the ranchers in the area were of Italian descent, so when he day worked in his youth, Italian food was served. Other areas he has worked ranches were owned by people of backgrounds adding a little bit of each ethnic group to his unique cooking style.

Currently Bob is day working on ranches out of Van Horn Texas. He lives there with his wife Catie and their son Dakota.

Catie is an artist with a website at http://www.ckinfordswest.com

For Cowboy Humor books by Bob visit http://www.2lazy4u.us

Bob also has cattle handling advice at http://www.naturalcattlehandling.com

They also host a cowboy poetry gathering with a format of being a cowboy entertainer talent show in Van Horn, Texas the first weekend in February. For more information visit http://www.texascrossroadscowboypoetry.org

7388613R0

Made in the USA
Charleston, SC
26 February 2011